AWAKENING
INNER LIGHT

EXPLORING THE DEPTHS OF THE SOUL
THROUGH THE WISDOM OF VIVEKANANDA

SOURISH DUTTA

To Narayan, the all-pervading God, who illuminates our path and guides us on our journey of self-discovery. To all the spiritual teachers who have shared their wisdom and inspired us to seek the truth within. And to NotionPress Publishers, who have helped bring these teachings to light and made them available to seekers everywhere. This book is dedicated with gratitude and reverence for the transformative power of yoga philosophy.

Contents

Foreword

As a lifelong seeker and practitioner of bhakti yoga philosophy, I am honoured to have the opportunity to write the foreword for "Awakening Inner Light" by my beloved child Sourish Dutta. From an early age, he has been deeply drawn to the teachings of Swami Vivekananda, and has dedicated his life to sharing this wisdom with others.

Through "Awakening Inner Light", Sourish offers a beautiful and inspiring guide to the teachings of karma yoga and jnana yoga, illuminating the path to inner peace, self-awareness, and spiritual growth. Drawing on Vivekananda's timeless wisdom and his own extensive knowledge and experience, he provides clear and practical insights that can help readers connect with their true selves and live with purpose and meaning.

I have watched with pride and admiration as Sourish has developed his expertise in yoga philosophy.

I offer my deepest thanks to Sourish for writing this book, and to NotionPress Publishers for helping to bring it to fruition. May "Awakening Inner Light" be a source of guidance and inspiration for all those who seek to awaken their inner light and live with love, joy, and purpose.

With all my love,
Soma Pal

Preface

As a lover of ancient Hindu philosophy and a student of Swami Vivekananda, I have long been drawn to the timeless wisdom of texts like the Bhagavad Gita and the ancient Puranas. These teachings provide a powerful framework for understanding the nature of reality, the purpose of life, and the true self. They offer guidance for cultivating self-awareness, compassion, and devotion, and for living with purpose and joy.

Through my studies, I have been inspired by the life and teachings of Swami Vivekananda, one of the great spiritual masters of the modern era. His vision and insights on karma yoga and jnana yoga have been particularly meaningful to me, offering a path to inner peace, wisdom, and liberation.

In "Awakening Inner Light", I have distilled some of the most profound teachings of Hindu philosophy and Swami Vivekananda's wisdom on karma yoga and jnana yoga, offering a guide that can help readers connect with their true selves and live with purpose and meaning. Through this book, I hope to inspire young readers to discover the transformative power of these teachings, and to see the relevance and beauty of ancient wisdom in our modern world.

I offer my deepest thanks to Swami Vivekananda for his profound insights and inspiration, and to all the ancient sages and teachers who have shared their wisdom with the world. I also express my gratitude to NotionPress Publishers for helping to make this book a reality.

May "Awakening Inner Light" be a source of guidance and inspiration for all those who seek to awaken their inner light and live with love, wisdom, and joy.

With love and reverence,
Sourish Dutta

Acknowledgements

I am grateful to Narayana, the all-pervading god, for his divine grace and inspiration, which have guided me throughout the process of writing this book.

I would like to express my deepest appreciation to my mother, Soma Pal, for instilling in me a love of learning and spirituality from a young age. Her unwavering support and encouragement have been a source of strength and inspiration to me throughout my life.

I would also like to thank my better half, Madhushree, for her love, support, and understanding during the many long hours I spent writing and editing this book. Her unwavering support and encouragement have been a source of strength and inspiration to me throughout my life.

Finally, I would like to extend my heartfelt thanks to all of the teachers, mentors, friends, and family members who have helped and encouraged me on this journey. Your wisdom, guidance, and encouragement have been invaluable to me, and I am honoured to have you all in my life.

With deepest gratitude,
Sourish Dutta

Prologue

असतो मा सद्गमय तमसो मा ज्योतिर्गमय मृत्योर्मा अमृतं गमय॥

Translation: "Lead me from the unreal to the real, from darkness to light, from death to immortality.

Swami Vivekananda, a renowned Hindu monk and one of the greatest spiritual leaders of the 19th century, is known for his profound teachings on Karma Yoga and Jnana Yoga. His teachings continue to inspire and guide people around the world, even more than a century after his passing.

Karma Yoga is the path of action, which emphasizes the importance of performing one's duties selflessly and without attachment to the results. Through selfless service, one can purify the mind and attain a state of detachment that is necessary for spiritual growth. Swami Vivekananda believed that Karma Yoga is a powerful tool for achieving spiritual liberation and breaking free from the cycle of birth and death.

Jnana Yoga, on the other hand, is the path of knowledge, which emphasizes the importance of self-inquiry and contemplation. By reflecting on the nature of the self and the universe, one can gain a deeper understanding of the ultimate reality. This knowledge can then help one transcend the limitations of the individual ego and attain a state of oneness with the universe.

Swami Vivekananda's teachings on Karma Yoga and Jnana Yoga are not limited to a particular religion or culture. They are universal and can be applied by people from all walks of life. His teachings on these paths can help people attain inner peace, wisdom, and a deeper sense of purpose.

In this book, we will explore some of Swami Vivekananda's most profound teachings on Karma Yoga and Jnana Yoga. We will look at how these teachings can be applied in our daily lives to help us achieve spiritual growth and enlightenment. Whether you are new to these paths or have been practicing them for years, this book will provide you with valuable insights and inspiration.

As you read this book, I invite you to keep an open mind and heart. May Swami Vivekananda's teachings on Karma Yoga and Jnana Yoga inspire you to embark on a journey of self-discovery and spiritual growth. May this book serve as a guide and source of inspiration as you navigate the ups and downs of life and seek to realize your true nature.

CHAPTER ONE

Karma Yoga

The Karma Yoga

Text 1. *Take up one idea. Make that one idea your life – think of it, dream of it, and live on that idea. Let the brain, muscles, nerves, and every part of your body, be full of that idea alone. This is the way to success that is the way great spiritual giants are produced.*

Explanation: One particular goal is very much needed to excel in any phase of your life. Your mind will provide you with several thoughts, emotions, and feelings for different occupations, for different goals and targets, yet it will be only you who could detect that one idea to which you want to give your whole life energy. The nature of the idea is not important, it means it may be spiritual or material. Although the idea must align with righteousness, the act and idea should be of truth and without selfish motives. In this material world, if you need success or material prosperity, then also you should have one single idea. I must say that having only a single idea will not help you until you are not executing your idea. The execution should also be perfect. It must be based on moral grounds and you should stand by the truth and nothing else. Again, morality changes with border and area. The morality which is prevalent in India, may not be prevalent in other states. Some acts are ideal for a Hindu whereas it is not for some other religion. Your idea should aim toward universal unity and universal morality. For instance, the Vedanta teaches about universal unity and diversification whereas many religions say that only their path is the only path to God. "Think of it, dream of it, and live on that idea" – we need to understand the profoundness of this statement. First, you should all know that Swami Vivekananda was a great Vedantist. Every word which came out of his mouth is based on the holy teachings of Vedanta. Swamiji told every word which resembles Vedanta. The level on which he was at that time, cannot be described in words. So, if anyone thinks that "Think of it, dream of it, and live on that idea" – those words refer to something materialistic attitude, then he or she is completely wrong. Briefly speaking, if anyone thought, and applies those motivating words to his materialistic goals, then also he will succeed but Swamiji was not on the side of that approach.

In reality, those words refer to the basics of Karma Yoga. Everyone should have one idea in which he shall invest his life yet he should be detached from the results. He shall not work for selfish motives. Because a normal human being doesn't know his true Self. He thinks that his ego and mind are what he is. But sadly, it is not. Selfish motives and uncontrolled desires, lead one to distress and hindrances; one forgets his real identity and starts working like an animal.

Now someone may ask that if we don't think about results then we will not be able to achieve the goal we set. The questioner is confused between the goal and results and attachment to it. The aim is what you have selected. To achieve that aim you should work incessantly. In this process, your total focus should be on your goal and not on your results which depends on your workings. Because if you do the work carefully, working day and night then your result will automatically come out great otherwise not. So, why waste time thinking about results? Another thing to notice is that when you get your result you will use it for the benefit of your close ones, but should you be attached to those results? No, you should not, because attachment will cause a great hindrance to your growth. Whether the result is positive or negative, you should not be attached to it. For example, a good result can make you so happy and attached to it that you may not get the preferred results next time, on the other hand, a failure can make you so demotivated that you may leave your dream or can make you powerless, which is equal to death.

The detachment towards the results should not make you inert towards working for your goals. Many of us today think that to be detached from the results of our work we should not work, work with lethargy, or be inactive in our duty. That is not the right attitude. Right from Jagadguru Adi Shankaracharya to Swami Vivekananda, everyone has followed this process to achieve their goal. People have a wrong notion that spiritual giants who had turned the impossible into possible, did that because of their luck. Normally, people also think that only selfish and materialistic people can change the world or only they can achieve their goals, and if one does act selflessly then he can do nothing. But that is a wrong assumption. Spiritual giants like Swami Vivekananda, Adi Shankaracharya, Shri Madhvacharya, and Shri Ramanujacharya, had done so much for mankind, for our spiritual benefit. You can also take the example of the founder Acharya of ISKCON, Srila Prabhupada, who had only forty rupees in his pocket and travelled to the west at the request of his guru. In his lifetime only, he built more than a hundred temples all over the world. Any sane person can learn many qualities from them. It is Adi Shankaracharya who re-established the values and principles of Upanishads and the Hindu view of life. It was those Vaishnav Acharyas who had re-established the Bhakti movement. It was Swami Vivekananda who introduced the world to Vedanta. Having one goal in our mind and working incessantly to achieve that with a detachment to results, can give us the ultimate results. Only by working like this, you can realize God. Only working in this way would not entail you, Work is worship if it is done as Niskama Karma Yoga. Working like this will make you mentally, physically, and spiritually strong.

Text 2. *"In a day, when you don't come across any problems – you can be sure that you are traveling in the wrong path."*

Explanation: The path of truth is always hard. When I remember the lives of Kauravas, the hundred sinful brothers, they always made the lives of Pandavas very much painful. They, themselves had a beautiful kingdom, prosperity, power, and everything yet they were jealous of Pandavas. But when Karma decided to return the debt with interest, Kauravas got destroyed and Pandavas got the kingdom back. The path of dharma is very difficult when you see it from the outside. But if you follow it, it will become easy and peaceful for you. The short time benefit and happiness may entail your suffering, but following dharma would seem like a difficult job yet it will bring you tranquillity. Here Swamiji explains the path of dharma and truth, the path of righteousness. It is always difficult in the beginning because our mind travels so fast towards short time benefits and enjoyment. A ten-hour long study is not comfortable but watching four movies one by one in a single day, is very much comfortable for many. Examples always have some shortcomings but do understand the point.

Now one may think that if the path of truth is hard and full of suffering then why do we need to go to that path? Why don't we simply enjoy life? The answer to this question is: You still don't know who wants to enjoy life. Is it you who wants to enjoy or is it your mind who wants it? Until and unless we get to know the real truth of this 'Self', we couldn't progress. Without restraining your senses and mind, it is obvious that your various acts of yours are going to entail you suffering and happiness, and distress in life. And if someone thinks that it is human life; the sufferings and happiness make life beautiful and meaningful then also it is an unnecessary argument. Because the purpose of human life is to realize its importance. Self-realization is necessary. We are spending our valuable human life and getting a sophisticated animal life. There are many things for human beings apart from eating, sleeping, mating, and defending. Problems will always come in your way of achieving your targets, they may be good or bad, and both are dangerous. But by observing those problems you can understand that you are progressing in your life. Don't leave Dharma and Satya.

Text 3: *"Be not afraid of anything, you will do Marvellous work. It is fearlessness that brings Heaven even in a moment."*

Explanation: Fear is our greatest enemy. It restricts our true potential to work selflessly and to serve people. Even in our materialistic journey, you will not attract achievements if you fear. Whenever we commence some new things, we fear it because of failure. But it is fear alone which brings the failure sooner. But we should keep in mind that every failure which is happening around you is because of your fear, rather there are many aspects to consider while discussing about failure. The most prominent thing which is involved is Law of Karma.

Text 4: **"Comfort is no test of truth. Truth is often far from being comfortable."**

Explanation: Simply because something is comfortable or feels good, it doesn't necessarily mean that it's true. In other words, our feelings of comfort and ease cannot be relied upon as a means of determining the accuracy of a statement or belief. Truth can often be challenging, difficult, and uncomfortable. It can challenge our beliefs and assumptions, and force us to confront difficult realities. But it is important to seek out the truth regardless of how it makes us feel, as this can lead to growth and a better understanding of the world around us. Confronting this truth might be uncomfortable, but it is important for the individual to acknowledge it in order to grow and improve themselves.

Text 5: **"The fire that warms us can also consume us; it is not the fault of the fire."**

Explanation: This refers to the dual nature of things that can bring both benefit and harm. The fire in the quote is a metaphor for anything that has the potential to positively impact our lives, but also carries the risk of causing harm.

The point being made is that the potential for harm is not inherent in the object or situation itself, but rather in the way that it is used. Just as fire can be used to warm us and provide light, it can also cause destruction if not properly managed. Similarly, other things like power, wealth, and technology can provide great benefits, but can also lead to negative consequences if not used responsibly.

The quote serves as a reminder that we must be mindful of the potential consequences of our actions and the things we use. We should be aware of the risks involved and take steps to minimize them, rather than blaming the object or situation itself.

In conclusion, the quote highlights the importance of being mindful of the dual nature of things in our lives and taking responsibility for the outcomes of our actions. Rather than blaming the fire, or any other positive and potentially harmful thing, we must recognize our own role in determining the impact it has on our lives.

Text 6: **"We are not what our thoughts have made us; so take care about what you think. Words are secondary. Thoughts live; They travel far."**

Explanation: It is emphasizing the power of our thoughts and beliefs. The quote suggests that our thoughts have a significant impact on who we are and how we view the world. It reminds us that we should be mindful of what we think and pay attention to the beliefs and thoughts that we hold.

The idea is that our thoughts shape our experiences and influence our actions, and therefore, it is important to be intentional and deliberate about what we think. The words we use are only a secondary expression of our thoughts and beliefs, and the real power lies in the thoughts themselves.

The phrase "thoughts live; they travel far" highlights the idea that our thoughts are not static and have the ability to spread and influence others. This is why it is important to be mindful of what we think and to be intentional about the beliefs that we hold, as they can have a lasting impact on our lives and the lives of others.

In conclusion, the quote is a reminder of the power of our thoughts and beliefs, and the importance of taking care about what we think. By being intentional and deliberate about our thoughts, we can shape our experiences and the world around us in a positive way.

Text 7: **"They alone live who lives for others."**

Explanation: The purpose and meaning of life can be found in serving others and making a positive impact on the world. The idea is that those who live for themselves alone, focused solely on their own wants and needs, will not find true fulfilment and satisfaction in life. Instead, it is through serving others and making a difference in the lives of others that one can truly live.

The quote is often attributed to Mahatma Gandhi, who believed in the importance of serving others and working towards the greater good. For Gandhi, the purpose of life was to help others and make the world a better place, rather than seeking personal gain or success.

The quote emphasizes the idea that living for others can bring a sense of purpose and meaning to one's life. It suggests that we can find joy and fulfilment in making a positive difference in the world, and that this is the true definition of a life well-lived.

In conclusion, the quote "They alone live who live for others" highlights the importance of serving others and making a positive impact on the world. By focusing on the needs and well-being of others, we can find purpose and meaning in our lives, and truly live.

Text 8: **"All power is within you, you can do, anything and everything. Believe in that do not believe that you are weak. You can do everything without even the guidance of anyone. Stand up express the divinity within you."**

Explanation: The quote expresses the idea of self-empowerment and encourages individuals to believe in their own abilities and to trust in the power within themselves.

Swami Vivekananda was a strong advocate of this idea, and his life was a testament to the power of self-belief and determination. Despite facing many challenges and obstacles, including poverty and discrimination, he went on to become a respected spiritual teacher and leader, inspiring millions of people around the world with his teachings.

Through his teachings, Swami Vivekananda encouraged individuals to find their own inner strength and to believe in themselves, regardless of their background or circumstances. He believed that everyone has the potential to achieve great things, and that it is only by tapping into the power within themselves that they can truly succeed.

The quote "All power is within you" is a reminder of this message, and encourages individuals to trust in their own abilities and to take control of their lives. By recognizing and expressing the divinity within themselves, individuals can achieve great things and fulfil their true potential.

In conclusion, the quote highlights the ideas of self-empowerment and self-belief that were central to Swami Vivekananda's teachings and life. By recognizing the power within themselves and expressing their own inner divinity, individuals can overcome challenges and achieve great things, just as Swami Vivekananda did.

Text 9: **"Ask nothing, want nothing in return. Give what you have to give; it will come back to you, but do not think of that now."**

Explanation: The quote expresses the idea of selfless giving, or the act of giving without expecting anything in return. Srila Prabhupada taught that true happiness and fulfilment can be found in giving, and that the act of giving should be done without any ulterior motives or expectations.

In his life, Srila Prabhupada demonstrated this idea through his own actions. He devoted himself to spreading the teachings of Krishna Consciousness, without asking for anything in return. Through his tireless efforts, he inspired countless individuals to adopt a more selfless and giving way of life.

The phrase "it will come back to you" suggests that the law of cause and effect applies to our actions, and that if we give selflessly, the good deeds will eventually come back to us. However, Srila Prabhupada emphasizes that the focus should be on giving and helping others, rather than on the potential rewards that may come in the future.

In conclusion, the quote highlights the ideas of selfless giving and selflessness that were central to Srila Prabhupada teachings and life. By giving without any expectations or motives, individuals can find true happiness and fulfilment, just as Srila Prabhupada did through his own life of service and devotion.

Text 10: **"Do one thing at a time, and while doing it put your whole soul into it to the exclusion of all else."**

Explanation: It emphasizes the importance of single-minded focus and concentration. It suggests that in order to achieve true excellence in anything we do, we must give our full attention and energy to the task at hand, rather than dividing our attention between multiple tasks or distractions.

One famous person who embodies this idea is the legendary inventor and entrepreneur, Thomas Edison. Edison is often described as being a master of focus and concentration, and was known for his ability to work long hours and remain fully absorbed in his work, even in the face of obstacles and setbacks. He famously said, "Genius is one percent inspiration and ninety-nine percent perspiration", reflecting his belief in the importance of hard work and focused effort in achieving success.

Edison's relentless focus and determination are often cited as key factors in his numerous inventions and innovations, including the development of the practical incandescent light bulb, the phonograph, and the motion picture camera. He believed that in order to achieve greatness, it was necessary to be fully immersed in the task at hand, and to put in the time and effort required to see it through to completion.

In conclusion, the quote "Do one thing at a time, and while doing it put your whole soul into it to the exclusion of all else" reflects the idea that true excellence and success come from giving our full attention and energy to the task at hand. The example of Thomas Edison demonstrates how this approach can lead to great achievements, even in the face of obstacles and setbacks.

Text 11: **"Whatever you think you will be. If you think yourself weak, weak you will be; if you think yourself strong, you will be."**

Explanation: It expresses the idea that our thoughts and beliefs about ourselves have a significant impact on our behaviour and outcomes. This idea is rooted in the concept of self-efficacy, or the belief in one's own ability to succeed in specific situations.

According to this perspective, if a person believes that they are weak or incapable, they are more likely to engage in behaviours that reinforce that belief and limit their potential for success. On the other hand, if a person believes in their own strength and ability, they are more likely to take on challenges, persist in the face of obstacles, and ultimately achieve their goals.

An example of a failure person who embodies this idea is the late Steve Jobs, co-founder of Apple Inc. Jobs was known for his innovative ideas and relentless pursuit of excellence, but he also experienced several setbacks and failures throughout his career. Despite these setbacks, Jobs never lost his belief in his own abilities, and he continued to take on new challenges and push the boundaries of technology and design.

In 1997, Jobs was forced out of Apple and founded NeXT Computer, a company that developed innovative computer software. Despite initial setbacks, Jobs' unwavering belief in himself and his team eventually led to the success of NeXT, which was later acquired by Apple and became the foundation for many of Apple's most popular products.

In conclusion, the quote "Whatever you think you will be. If you think yourself weak, weak you will be; if you think yourself strong, you will be" highlights the importance of our thoughts and beliefs in shaping our behaviour and outcomes. The example of Steve Jobs demonstrates how a person's belief in their own abilities can influence their success, even in the face of failure and setbacks.

Text 12: **"Anything that makes you weak – physically, intellectually and spiritually, reject it as poison."**

Explanation: We should be proactive in avoiding things that negatively impact our health, well-being, and overall development. This can refer to physical habits such as substance abuse, intellectual pursuits that undermine our growth and learning, or spiritual practices that detract from our inner peace and happiness.

The phrase "reject it as poison" is a metaphor that highlights the dangers of allowing these harmful influences into our lives. Just as poison can weaken or harm our physical bodies, so too can negative experiences and practices weaken our minds and spirits. The quote suggests that we should be discerning and choose to avoid anything that has a negative impact on our overall well-being.

This idea can be applied in a number of ways. For example, it could mean rejecting unhealthy habits such as smoking, excessive drinking, or drug use, as these can have a profound impact on our physical health. It could also mean avoiding negative relationships or toxic environments that drain our energy and happiness, as these can affect our mental and emotional well-being.

Ultimately, the quote "Anything that makes you weak – physically, intellectually and spiritually, reject it as poison" is a reminder that we have the power to shape our lives and our experiences. By being mindful of the things that negatively impact our well-being and making conscious choices to avoid them, we can cultivate strength, health, and happiness in all aspects of our lives.

Text 13: **"Whatever we wish to be in future can be produced by our present actions; so we have to know how to act."**

Explanation: Our future selves and circumstances are largely shaped by the choices and actions we take in the present moment. This means that if we want to achieve a particular goal or outcome, we need to take the right steps and make the right decisions today.

This idea is rooted in the concept of cause and effect, where our choices and actions today determine the consequences that will follow in the future. In other words, the seeds that we plant today , will determine the crops we reap tomorrow.

For example, consider a person who wants to become a successful entrepreneur. They know that this goal requires hard work, determination, and a willingness to take risks. To achieve this goal, they need to be mindful of the actions they take today, such as seeking out educational opportunities, networking with successful businesspeople, and making smart investments. These actions will lay the foundation for the success they hope to achieve in the future.

In conclusion, the quote "Whatever we wish to be in future can be produced by our present actions; so, we have to know how to act" highlights the importance of being intentional and purposeful in our choices and actions. By being mindful of the impact our decisions today will have on our future selves and circumstances, we can create the lives and outcomes that we desire.

Text 14: **"Learn everything that is good from others, but bring it in, and in your own way absorb it; do not become others."**

Explanation: Emphasizes the importance of learning from others while maintaining one's own individuality and unique perspective. The message is that we should be open to learning from the experiences, insights, and perspectives of others, but we should not simply imitate or copy them. Instead, we should take what we have learned and incorporate it into our own lives in a way that is authentic and true to who we are.

One example of this approach can be seen in the life of Ramanujacharya, a Hindu philosopher and theologian who lived in South India in the 11th century. Ramanujacharya was a prolific writer and teacher who was highly influenced by the teachings of the Bhagavad Gita and other Hindu scriptures. He was also deeply influenced by the works of other philosophers and theologians of his time.

Despite this, Ramanujacharya did not simply adopt their ideas and perspectives uncritically. Instead, he carefully considered their teachings and incorporated them into his own philosophy and teachings in a way that was authentic and true to his own beliefs and understanding.

Through his writing and teaching, Ramanujacharya helped to establish the Sri Vaishnava tradition, which remains one of the largest and most influential schools of Hindu philosophy to this day. He also made important contributions to Hindu theology and ethics, and his legacy continues to be celebrated and studied by scholars and devotees around the world.

In conclusion, the quote "Learn everything that is good from others, but bring it in, and in your own way absorb it; do not become others" encourages us to be open-minded and receptive to the ideas and perspectives of others, while also being true to ourselves and maintaining our own unique identities and individuality. The example of Ramanujacharya demonstrates how this approach can lead to personal growth and development, as well as make a lasting impact on the world around us.

Text 15: **"Arise, awake, stop not until your goal is reached."**

Explanation: It is a call to action and a reminder of the importance of perseverance and determination in pursuing one's goals. The message is that we should not let setbacks, obstacles, or difficulties deter us from working towards our goals, but instead, we should be resolute and relentless in our efforts to achieve them.

One example of this approach can be seen in the life of Netaji Subhas Chandra Bose, a prominent Indian nationalist leader who fought against British rule in India during the first half of the 20th century. Bose was a charismatic and influential figure who was committed to the cause of Indian independence and worked tirelessly to mobilize public support for the independence movement.

Despite facing numerous challenges and setbacks, including arrest and imprisonment, Bose never wavered in his commitment to his goals. He continued to organize and lead anti-British campaigns, and he eventually went abroad to seek support from other nations for the independence movement.

Bose's efforts ultimately paid off, and he played a significant role in raising international awareness of the Indian independence movement and building support for the cause. Today, he is remembered as one of India's greatest heroes and a symbol of resistance against colonial oppression.

In conclusion, the quote "Arise, awake, stop not until your goal is reached" inspires us to be persistent and determined in our pursuit of our goals, regardless of the obstacles and difficulties we may face. The example of Netaji Subhas Chandra Bose demonstrates the power of this approach and the impact that one person can have when they are dedicated and relentless in their efforts.

Text 16: **"The cheerful mind perseveres and the strong mind hews its way through a thousand difficulties."**

Explanation: It highlights the importance of a positive and resilient attitude in overcoming challenges and obstacles. It suggests that a person with a cheerful and optimistic outlook will be more likely to persist in their efforts and find success, even in the face of difficulties.

This quote reflects the idea that the right state of mind can be a powerful tool in overcoming obstacles and achieving one's goals. It suggests that a positive attitude and determination can help us push through adversity and emerge stronger on the other side.

The phrase "hews its way through a thousand difficulties" suggests that the strong mind is like a sharp tool that cuts through obstacles, rather than being stopped or discouraged by them. This image conveys the idea that a person with a strong and resolute mind will find a way to overcome any obstacle, no matter how difficult.

In conclusion, this quote encourages us to adopt a positive and determined outlook, even in the face of challenges and difficulties. By maintaining a cheerful and strong mind, we can persevere and achieve our goals, despite the obstacles that may arise.

Text 17: **"Astrology and all these mystical things are generally signs of a weak mind; therefore, as soon as they are becoming prominent in our minds, we should see a physician, take good food, and rest."**

Explanation: This is a critique of relying on mystical or supernatural beliefs to solve life's problems. The quote suggests that people who turn to such beliefs as a means of finding solace or answers to their problems are likely suffering from a weak mind, and that they should focus on more practical solutions, such as seeking medical advice and taking care of their physical health through good nutrition and rest.

One example of this approach can be seen in the teachings of Swami Vivekananda, a Hindu monk and teacher who was active in the late 19th and early 20th centuries. Vivekananda was a strong advocate of rational thinking and self-empowerment, and he emphasized the importance of using our own efforts and abilities to solve life's problems, rather than relying on supernatural beliefs or outside forces.

In his teachings, Vivekananda encouraged people to focus on developing their own inner strength and abilities, rather than seeking solace in mystical or supernatural beliefs. He believed that by developing our own minds and bodies, we can overcome any obstacle and achieve our goals, without relying on external forces or mystical beliefs.

In conclusion, the quote "Astrology and all these mystical things are generally signs of a weak mind" is a reminder that practical and self-directed solutions are often more effective than relying on mystical or supernatural beliefs. The example of Swami Vivekananda demonstrates the importance of this approach, and the impact that it can have on personal growth and empowerment.

Text 18: **"The Tapas and the other Yoga that were practiced in other Yugas do not work now. What is needed in this Yuga is giving, helping others."**

Explanation: It refers to the idea that the spiritual practices and disciplines that were effective in ancient times may not be as effective in the present era. The Hindu tradition recognizes different "Yugas," or ages, each with its own set of spiritual and cultural practices that are appropriate for that time period.

According to this quote, the current Yuga (age) is characterized by a greater emphasis on selfless service and helping others, rather than traditional spiritual practices like Tapas (austerities) or other forms of Yoga. This idea aligns with the broader Hindu tradition of living a life of compassion and selflessness, where the well-being of others is valued over one's own personal gain.

This view emphasizes the importance of putting others before oneself and using one's resources, time, and skills to help those in need. It suggests that the greatest spiritual progress can be made not through personal asceticism or spiritual pursuits, but through actively serving and helping others.

In Hinduism, this ideal of selfless service is embodied by figures like Lord Krishna, who is revered for his devotion to helping others and their willingness to put others' needs before his own. This ideal is also reflected in practices like seva (selfless service) and dana (charity), which are considered key aspects of Hindu spiritual life.

In conclusion, the quote "The Tapas and the other Yoga that were practiced in other Yugas do not work now. What is needed in this Yuga is giving, helping others" reflects the Hindu tradition of valuing compassion and selfless service as a key aspect of spiritual growth. This view emphasizes the importance of using our resources, time, and skills to help others, rather than relying solely on personal spiritual practices.

Text 19: **"Condemn none, if you can stretch out a helping hand, do so. If you cannot, fold your hands, bless your brothers, and let them go their own way."**

Explanation: It is a statement that encourages a non-judgmental and supportive approach to others. It suggests that instead of criticizing or condemning people, one should try to assist them if they are able to, and if not, then simply bless them and let them make their own choices and decisions. Adi Shankaracharya's life is an example of the principle expressed in the quote "Condemn none, if you can stretch out a helping hand, do so. If you cannot, fold your hands, bless your brothers, and let them go their own way." He approached all people with compassion and respect, regardless of their religion, caste, or beliefs. He encouraged his followers to see the divine in all things and to work towards the ultimate goal of liberation for all beings. Through his teachings and example, he demonstrated that one can live a life of compassion and non-judgment, always offering a helping hand to those in need and blessing those who choose to go their own way.

Text 20: **"Our duty is to encourage everyone in his struggle to live up to his own highest idea, and strive at the same time to** make the ideal as near as possible."

Explanation: This statement means that it is our responsibility to support and motivate others in their pursuit of fulfilling their personal aspirations and goals. At the same time, we should also strive to bring our own ideals closer to reality. Swami Vivekananda was known for his deep devotion to God and his commitment to serving humanity. He encouraged people to strive for their highest potential and to live a life of service to others. Through his speeches and teachings, he inspired millions of people to awaken their spiritual awareness and to live according to their highest ideals.

Swami Vivekananda travelled extensively throughout India and the world, spreading his message of hope, peace, and unity. He encouraged people to see the divine within themselves and to work towards the betterment of all humanity. Through his own actions and teachings, he lived up to his own highest ideal of a life dedicated to service and spirituality, and inspired others to do the same.

Text 21: **"The will is not free – it is a phenomenon bound by cause and effect – but there is something behind the will which is free."**

Explanation: This statement suggests that the human will, or the ability to make choices and decisions, is not independent or unconditioned. Rather, it is influenced by various causes and conditions, such as past experiences, emotions, cultural and societal norms, and so on. However, the statement also implies that there is something beyond the will, a deeper aspect of our being, that is free from these limitations.

In philosophical terms, this could be interpreted as the distinction between the surface level of consciousness, which is conditioned and limited by various factors, and the deeper, unchanging aspect of consciousness, which is often referred to as the Self, Atman, or the soul. This deeper aspect of consciousness is believed to be free from the limitations of the ego and the limitations of cause and effect.

In this perspective, the will can be seen as a reflection of the underlying motivations, desires, and intentions that are shaped by the conditioning of the mind and the body. However, behind the will lies the true self, which is pure, unchanging, and free from the limitations of time and space. By accessing this deeper aspect of our being and tapping into our true nature, we can gain greater clarity, wisdom, and freedom in our choices and actions.

Text 22: **"Devotion to duty is the highest form of worship of God."**

Explanation: Devotion to duty refers to being fully dedicated and committed to fulfilling your responsibilities and obligations. When someone is devoted to their duty, they put their full effort into it and make sure they are doing their best.

This concept is considered the highest form of worship of God because it shows that a person is putting their faith into action. By fulfilling their duties, they are demonstrating their belief in God and their respect for His laws and commandments. It also shows that they are using the abilities and opportunities given to them by God for the betterment of themselves and others.

For example, if someone has a duty to care for their family, and they do so with love and dedication, they are not only fulfilling their responsibilities but also showing their devotion to God. Similarly, if a person has a job and they perform their duties with diligence and integrity, they are demonstrating their devotion to God through their work.

In summary, devotion to duty is considered the highest form of worship of God because it is a tangible way of demonstrating one's faith and respect for God's laws. By fulfilling their duties with love, dedication, and effort, a person is showing their devotion to God in a practical and meaningful way.

Text 23: **"If money help a man to do good to others, it is of some value; but if not, it is simply a mass of evil, and the sooner it is got rid of, the better."**

Explanation: This quote is emphasizing the idea that money is only valuable if it is used to do good for others. If money is not used in this way, it is considered a "mass of evil." This means that it is not only useless, but it also has negative consequences and may cause harm.

The idea is that money should not be valued for its own sake, but for what it can help a person accomplish. If a person uses their money to help others, for example, by making charitable donations or supporting those in need, then their money has value and is being used in a positive way. On the other hand, if a person uses their money for selfish or harmful purposes, such as exploiting others or contributing to negative social or environmental outcomes, then the money is not serving a positive purpose and may actually be causing harm.

An example of this idea in practice is a wealthy individual who uses their money to support various charitable organizations. This person is using their wealth to do good for others, and their money is therefore of some value. In contrast, if the same individual were to use their money to fund illegal or unethical activities, their money would be a "mass of evil" and would not be serving a positive purpose.

In conclusion, this quote is emphasizing the idea that money should be valued based on how it is used, and that it is only truly valuable if it is used to do good for others. Money that is not used in this way is considered to be a "mass of evil."

Text 24: **"Never think there is anything impossible for the soul. It is the greatest heresy to think so. If there is sin, this is the only sin; to say that you are weak, or others are weak."**

Explanation: The quote is emphasizing the idea that it is a mistake, or "heresy," to believe that anything is impossible for the soul. According to Bhagat Singh, the only sin is to believe that you or others are weak.

The idea is that the soul has unlimited potential and that any limitations or obstacles that exist are only in our minds. By believing in our own limitations or the limitations of others, we limit our own potential and limit what we can accomplish. However, if we believe in the unlimited potential of the soul, then we can overcome any obstacles and achieve great things.

Bhagat Singh was an example of this philosophy in practice. Despite facing significant opposition and adversity in his efforts to fight for Indian independence, he never lost faith in his cause or in his own abilities. Through his unwavering commitment and belief in the unlimited potential of the soul, he was able to inspire others and make significant contributions to the independence movement.

In conclusion, Bhagat Singh believed that it is a mistake to believe that anything is impossible for the soul. By believing in our own or others' limitations, we limit our own potential and limit what we can achieve. Instead, we should believe in the unlimited potential of the soul and strive to overcome any obstacles that may stand in our way.

Text 25: **"Are you unselfish? That is the question. If you are, you will be perfect without reading a single religious book, without going into a single church or temple."**

Explanation: This quote is emphasizing the idea that unselfishness is a key characteristic of a truly virtuous person, and that this quality can be achieved without relying on religious books or attending religious institutions. The suggestion is that unselfishness is not necessarily dependent on religious beliefs or practices, but is instead a reflection of a person's character and actions.

Unselfishness refers to a willingness to put the needs and interests of others before one's own. An unselfish person is someone who is considerate, compassionate, and generous, and who is motivated by a desire to help others and make a positive difference in the world.

Shri Ramakrishna lived a simple life, devoting himself to prayer, meditation, and service to others. He believed in the unity of all religions and taught that all paths lead to the same divine reality. Despite his own spiritual attainments, Shri Ramakrishna never lost his humility and compassion for others, and he was always ready to help those in need.

Shri Ramakrishna's teachings have inspired countless people and have had a profound impact on the spiritual life of India. He is revered by his followers for his selflessness, his devotion to God, and his compassion for others, and is considered to be a shining example of the power of unselfishness in making a positive impact on the world.

In conclusion, Shri Ramakrishna Paramhansa is another example of an unselfish personality who dedicated his life to serving others and making a positive difference in the world. His unwavering devotion to God and his selflessness in serving others serve as an inspiration to others and demonstrate the power of unselfishness in making a positive impact on the world.

Text 26: **"The land where humanity has attained its highest towards gentleness, towards generosity, towards purity, towards calmness – it is India."**

Explanation: The speaker is highlighting the fact that India has produced many great spiritual leaders and saints who embody the qualities of gentleness, generosity, purity, and calmness.

India is a land of great spiritual and cultural diversity, with a rich history that spans thousands of years. From ancient Hindu scriptures and meditation practices to the teachings of Buddha, India has always been a centre of spiritual knowledge and enlightenment. Throughout its history, India has produced many great spiritual leaders who have inspired and guided people from all walks of life, teaching them the importance of compassion, selflessness, and inner peace.

The gentle and peaceful nature of the Indian people, their generosity and hospitality, and their deep spiritual wisdom are all testament to the rich spiritual heritage of this great land. Whether you look to the teachings of the ancient sages, the life stories of modern saints, or the daily practices of ordinary people, it is clear that India has much to offer the world in terms of spiritual guidance and wisdom.

In conclusion, the quote "The land where humanity has attained its highest towards gentleness, towards generosity, towards purity, towards calmness – it is India" is a tribute to the rich spiritual and cultural heritage of India and to the many great spiritual leaders and saints who have called this land home. Whether you are a seeker of inner peace, a lover of rich cultural traditions, or simply someone looking to learn more about the human spirit, India is truly a land of great inspiration and beauty.

Text 27: **"First, believe in this world – that there is meaning behind everything."**

Explanation: Swami Vivekananda's quote, "First, believe in this world – that there is meaning behind everything," is a call to embrace a spiritual perspective on life. According to Swamiji, the key to living a fulfilling life is to have faith that everything in this world has a deeper purpose and meaning.

In the spiritual context, this quote encourages us to look beyond the material world and to see the divine hand that guides everything. Swamiji believed that everything in the universe, from the smallest particles to the grandest galaxies, is interconnected and part of a larger cosmic plan. He taught that by having faith in the underlying meaning behind everything, we can tap into a deeper source of wisdom and inspiration.

When we view the world through this spiritual lens, we can see the beauty and wonder in everything around us. We begin to understand that every event, every person, and every experience has a role to play in the greater scheme of things. This sense of purpose and meaning can bring a new level of peace and happiness to our lives.

Swamiji's message is that we don't need to search for meaning and purpose in life, as it is already there, waiting for us to discover it. By embracing a spiritual perspective and having faith in the underlying meaning of the world, we can transform our lives and find a deeper sense of fulfilment and contentment.

In conclusion, Swami Vivekananda's quote, "First, believe in this world – that there is meaning behind everything," encourages us to view the world through a spiritual lens and to have faith in the underlying purpose and meaning of everything. By embracing this perspective, we can tap into a deeper source of wisdom and find a new level of peace and happiness in our lives.

Text 28: **"We are so lazy; we do not want to do anything ourselves. We want a Personal God, a saviour or a Prophet to do everything for us."**

Explanation: The quote, "We are so lazy; we do not want to do anything ourselves. We want a Personal God, a saviour, or a Prophet to do everything for us," speaks to a common human tendency to rely on external sources for motivation and guidance, rather than taking responsibility for our own lives.

In the context of spirituality, this quote is a reminder that the path to enlightenment and personal growth requires effort and discipline. Rather than seeking a quick fix or a saviour to do everything for us, we must take an active role in our own spiritual development.

Swamiji is saying that we must be willing to do the work required to achieve our goals, whether they are spiritual, personal, or professional. This requires effort, commitment, and discipline, as well as the willingness to take risks and face challenges head-on.

However, this doesn't mean that we have to go it alone. In spirituality, there are many sources of guidance and support, including scripture, teachers, mentors, and like-minded community members. These resources can provide the encouragement, wisdom, and motivation that we need to stay on track and achieve our goals.

In conclusion, the quote "We are so lazy; we do not want to do anything ourselves. We want a Personal God, a saviour, or a Prophet to do everything for us" highlights the importance of taking responsibility for our own lives and spiritual development. While external support and guidance are important, true growth and enlightenment require effort, commitment, and discipline on our part. By embracing this mindset, we can unlock our full potential and achieve our highest aspirations.

Text 29: **"We have to go back to philosophy to treat things as they are. We are suffering from our own Karma. It is not the fault of God."**

Explanation: Karma is the concept that our actions, both in this life and in past lives, determine our current circumstances and future outcomes. According to this philosophy, we are responsible for our own experiences, and the suffering or joy we experience is a result of the actions we have taken.

The quote suggests that in order to understand and address our current challenges and struggles, we must turn to philosophy and understand the role that our own actions have played in creating our current circumstances. It implies that we should not look to external sources, such as God, to explain or fix our problems, but instead take responsibility for our own lives and work to improve our situation through our own actions.

For example, if a person is struggling with financial difficulties, they may blame their circumstances on a lack of support from God or the universe. However, according to the principle of karma, their financial difficulties may be a result of their own past actions, such as spending beyond their means or not saving for the future. In this scenario, the solution would not be to pray for a miracle, but to take practical steps to improve their financial situation, such as creating a budget and finding new sources of income.

In conclusion, the quote "We have to go back to philosophy to treat things as they are. We are suffering from our own Karma. It is not the fault of God," encourages us to take responsibility for our own lives and circumstances and to understand that our experiences are a result of our own actions, not external factors. By embracing this philosophy, we can empower ourselves to make positive changes and improve our lives.

Text 30: **"Who makes us ignorant? We ourselves. We put our hands over our eyes and weep that it is dark."**

Explanation: Swamiji, in this quote, is pointing out that ignorance is not imposed upon us by external forces, but rather it is a state that we create for ourselves. He says, "Who makes us ignorant? We ourselves. We put our hands over our eyes and weep that it is dark."

This quote suggests that we have the power to control our own level of knowledge and understanding, and that the ignorance we experience is a choice that we make. Swamiji is encouraging us to take responsibility for our own learning and growth, and not to blame external factors for our lack of knowledge.

For example, if a person is struggling with a certain subject in school, they may complain that the teacher is not good or the material is too difficult. However, Swamiji's perspective would be that it is the student's own responsibility to put in the effort to understand the material, and that if they truly want to learn, they will find a way.

In conclusion, Swamiji's quote "Who makes us ignorant? We ourselves. We put our hands over our eyes and weep that it is dark," is a reminder that we have the power to control our own level of understanding and knowledge, and that ignorance is a choice that we make. By taking responsibility for our own learning and growth, we can empower ourselves to overcome ignorance and achieve a deeper understanding of the world around us.

Text 31: **"We came to enjoy, we are being enjoyed. We came to rule, we are being ruled. We came to work, we are being worked. All the time, we find that. And this comes into every detail of our life."**

Explanation: This quote by Swamiji speaks to the idea that we may have our own intentions and plans, but in reality, we are often at the mercy of circumstances and external factors that shape our experiences and outcomes.

For example, someone might have come to a new city with the intention of enjoying a relaxing vacation, but upon arriving, he finds himself caught in the hustle and bustle of city life and is unable to find the peace and relaxation he sought. He realizes that, rather than being able to enjoy the city on his own terms, he is being enjoyed by the city itself.

Similarly, one may have come to a new job with the intention of ruling and taking control, but instead finds himself being ruled by his boss and company policies. He may have come to work with the intention of using his skills and abilities to contribute and make a difference, but instead finds himself being worked, with long hours and a heavy workload.

This idea is relevant to many aspects of our lives, and can be seen in how we interact with the world around us. The point being made is that we often have to adjust our expectations and adapt to the circumstances we find ourselves in, rather than imposing our will on the world.

Text 32: **"Stand upon the self, only then can we truly love the world. Take a very high stand; knowing our universal nature, we must look with perfect calmness upon all the panorama of the world."**

Explanation: This quote speaks to the philosophy of Vedanta, which is one of the ancient Hindu philosophical traditions. According to Vedanta, the ultimate reality is the Self or Atman, which is understood to be an eternal, unchanging essence that underlies all of creation.

The idea behind this quote is that in order to truly love and understand the world, we must first have a deep understanding of our own true nature as the Self. By standing upon the self, we are able to look upon the world with a sense of detachment and equanimity, seeing all things, both good and bad, as mere appearances that do not affect our true nature as the Self.

In Vedanta, it is believed that the world is an illusion or maya, created by our own ignorance and mistaken identity with the body and mind. By realizing our true nature as the Self, we are able to transcend this illusion and see the world as it truly is.

In this sense, standing upon the self is not just a matter of having a strong sense of self-esteem, but rather a recognition of our own infinite nature and our connection to the universal consciousness. This awareness allows us to see the world with compassion and love, recognizing that all beings are part of the same infinite consciousness and that their experiences are a reflection of our own.

So, this quote is inviting us to take a very high stand, to recognize our true nature as the Self, and to look upon the world with a calm and detached perspective, knowing that all of its appearances are ultimately fleeting and do not affect our true nature as the Self.

Text 33: **"It is the patient building of character, the intense struggle to realize the truth, which alone will tell in the future of humanity."**

Explanation: This quote highlights the importance of character building and the pursuit of truth in shaping the future of humanity. According to the ancient Hindu philosophical tradition, the ultimate goal of human existence is to attain self-realization and a deep understanding of the ultimate reality.

This is achieved through a process of self-discovery and inner growth, characterized by the patient building of character and the intense struggle to realize the truth. It is believed that this process involves a sustained effort to cultivate virtues such as compassion, honesty, and wisdom, and to overcome ignorance and delusion.

This tradition emphasizes that the ultimate truth can only be known through direct personal experience and cannot be grasped through mere intellectual understanding or external authority. It is through this process of self-discovery that individuals can attain a state of inner peace, clarity, and harmony with the world.

In this sense, the quote is emphasizing the idea that it is the individual effort to cultivate inner character and to pursue the truth that will have the greatest impact on the future of humanity. By transforming ourselves, we contribute to the transformation of the world and help to create a brighter and more enlightened future for all beings.

Text 34: **"Work and worship are necessary to take away the veil, to lift off the bondage and illusion."**

Explanation: This quote speaks to the idea that both work and worship are important elements in the path of self-realization and liberation from ignorance and delusion. The concept is often associated with Bhakti Yoga, one of the paths of yoga that emphasizes devotion and worship as a means of attaining union with the divine.

In Bhakti Yoga, worship and devotion to a personal deity or divine figure is seen as a means of purifying the mind and elevating consciousness. Through regular practice of worship, individuals can cultivate qualities such as devotion, love, and surrender, and develop a deeper understanding of the nature of the self and the ultimate reality.

Work, on the other hand, is seen as an opportunity to put spiritual principles into practice and to purify the mind and body. By performing work as an offering to the divine and by approaching work with a spirit of detachment and service, individuals can purify their actions and cultivate a deeper sense of inner peace and contentment.

A great example of this idea can be seen in the life and teachings of Shri Ramakrishna. Shri Ramakrishna emphasized the importance of both work and worship in the spiritual journey, encouraging his disciples to perform work as an offering to the divine and to approach all tasks, no matter how mundane, with a spirit of devotion and surrender. He taught that work and worship are complementary aspects of the spiritual path, and that each can help to support and deepen the other.

Text 35: **"To all of you, wherever there is an outbreak of plague or famine or whatever the people are in distress, and mitigate their sufferings. Preach this ideal from door to door, and you will yourselves be benefitted by it at the same time that you are doing good to your country."**

Explanation: This quote by Swamiji highlights the importance of serving others and alleviating the suffering of those in need. The reference to "an outbreak of plague or famine" suggests that Swamiji is emphasizing the importance of providing assistance to people during times of crisis and hardship.

The message is clear: to help others and to make a positive impact on the world, we must actively seek out opportunities to serve and to relieve the suffering of those in need. By doing so, we not only benefit those we are helping, but we also reap personal benefits in the form of inner satisfaction and a sense of fulfilment.

Swamiji encourages the listener to "preach this ideal from door to door," indicating that he believes that the message of service and compassion should be widely shared and embraced by all. In this sense, the quote can be seen as an invitation to actively participate in creating a better world by serving others and mitigating their suffering.

Overall, this quote is a reminder of the importance of serving others and making a positive impact on the world. By living this ideal and actively seeking out opportunities to serve, we can create a better future for ourselves, our communities, and the world at large.

Text 36: **"My hope of the future lies in the youths of character, intelligent, renouncing all for the service of others and obedient – good to themselves and the country at large."**

Explanation: This quote by Swamiji highlights the importance of character, intelligence, selflessness, and obedience in shaping the future. By emphasizing the role of the "youths," Swamiji is suggesting that young people have the potential to play a significant role in shaping the future and creating positive change in society.

Swamiji's hope for the future lies in young people who possess strong character, are intelligent, and are committed to serving others. He also emphasizes the importance of renouncing self-interest for the good of the community, indicating that selflessness and a spirit of service are essential qualities in creating a better future.

In terms of the youth population of India, as of 2021, approximately 63% of the country's population is below the age of 35, making India one of the youngest countries in the world. This large youth population presents a significant opportunity for the country to harness the potential of young people to drive positive change and contribute to the development of the nation.

Overall, this quote by Swamiji is a call to action for young people to cultivate the qualities of character, intelligence, selflessness, and obedience, and to use their potential to make a positive impact on society. By doing so, they can help to create a brighter and more prosperous future for themselves, their communities, and the world at large.

Text 37: **"It is very easy to point out the defects of institutions, all being more or less imperfect, but he is the real benefactor of humanity who helps the individual to overcome his imperfections under whatever institutions he may live."**

Explanation: This quote by Swamiji highlights the importance of personal transformation and growth as a means of creating positive change in society. While it is easy to criticize and point out the flaws of institutions and systems, true progress and benefits for humanity can only be achieved by focusing on the individual and helping them to overcome their own imperfections.

From a spiritual perspective, the quote can be understood as a reminder that true transformation and growth must come from within. By working to overcome our own limitations, weaknesses, and flaws, we can become better individuals and make a positive impact on the world around us.

In this sense, the quote is a call to action for individuals to take responsibility for their own personal growth and development, rather than solely relying on external institutions to provide solutions to societal problems. By cultivating inner strength, wisdom, and compassion, individuals can help to create a better world by spreading positivity, hope, and love to those around them.

Overall, this quote by Swamiji is a reminder that the key to creating a better world lies within each and every one of us. By focusing on our own personal growth and transformation, we can help to make a positive impact on the world and bring about a brighter future for all.

Text 38: **"Nothing will avail in our country without setting a glowing and living example before the people. What we want are some young men who will renounce everything and sacrifice their lives for their country's sake. We should first form their lives and then some real work can be expected."**

Explanation: This quote by Swamiji emphasizes the importance of setting a positive example and leading by example in order to bring about positive change in society. He believes that the key to creating a better future lies in the actions and behaviours of individuals, and that true progress can only be achieved by those who are willing to make sacrifices and work tirelessly for the benefit of others.

From the perspective of Karma Yoga, the quote can be understood as a call to action for individuals to live their lives in service to others, using their actions and behaviours to inspire and motivate others to do the same. Karma Yoga is a path of selfless action, where one performs actions not for personal gain, but for the greater good.

Swamiji's call for young men to "renounce everything and sacrifice their lives for their country's sake" is a reminder of the importance of making sacrifices and taking bold actions in order to bring about positive change. He believes that by setting a "glowing and living example" and forming their lives around selflessness and service, individuals can inspire others and bring about real and lasting change in the world.

Overall, this quote by Swamiji is a reminder of the power of individual actions and the importance of setting a positive example for others to follow. By practicing Karma Yoga and living a life of selfless service, individuals can help to bring about positive change in society and contribute to the betterment of the world.

Text 39: **"Do not dragged away out of this Indian life; do not for a moment think that it would be better for India if all the Indians dressed, ate, and behaved like another race."**

Explanation: This quote by Swamiji is a call for the preservation and celebration of Indian cultural heritage and identity. He is urging Indians not to abandon their cultural traditions and way of life in favour of imitating or adopting the customs and practices of other cultures.

Swamiji recognizes the unique qualities and strengths of Indian culture and believes that it is essential for Indians to maintain and preserve their cultural identity in order to maintain a strong and cohesive national identity. He believes that by embracing and celebrating their cultural heritage, Indians can remain connected to their roots, values, and traditions and pass these important cultural touchstones down to future generations.

The quote is also a reminder of the importance of cultural diversity and the value that different cultures and traditions can bring to the world. By embracing and celebrating our cultural differences, we can enrich and broaden our understanding of the world and each other, fostering greater cultural exchange and understanding.

Overall, this quote by Swamiji is a call for Indians to maintain and celebrate their cultural heritage, and to resist the temptation to abandon their traditions and way of life in favour of imitating others. By embracing their cultural identity, Indians can help to strengthen their national identity and contribute to the celebration of cultural diversity in the world.

Text 40: **"It is character that cleave through adamantine walls of difference."**

Explanation: This quote emphasizes the idea that a strong and virtuous character can help overcome obstacles and differences, regardless of how seemingly insurmountable they may be. The phrase "adamantine walls of difference" refers to the seemingly unbreakable barriers that can exist between individuals, such as differences in culture, race, ethnicity, religion, or nationality.

However, the quote suggests that a person with a strong and virtuous character, someone who possesses traits such as integrity, courage, and compassion, can help to break down these barriers and foster greater understanding and unity. In other words, a person with a strong character has the power to bring people together and bridge divides, even in the face of seemingly insurmountable obstacles.

One famous example of this is Nelson Mandela, the former president of South Africa. Despite facing decades of apartheid and racial segregation, Mandela was able to bring people together and help heal the divisions between different ethnic groups in his country. Through his tireless work to promote peace, reconciliation, and human rights, Mandela demonstrated the power of character to overcome differences and build bridges between communities.

Overall, this quote highlights the idea that a strong and virtuous character can help to overcome obstacles and differences, and that people with such a character can play an important role in promoting unity and understanding in the world.

Karma Yoga, according to Swami Vivekananda, is the path of action, where work is done with love and detachment. It is a way to realize the infinite potential that lies within each one of us. To succeed on this path, we must arise, awake, and not stop until the goal is reached. We must not wait for anyone or anything but do whatever we can with courage and fearlessness. In doing so, we will inevitably encounter challenges, but we must not be afraid of them, for all power is within us. Perfection is infinite, and we are the infinite already, striving to manifest that potential. The key is to conquer ourselves, and then the whole universe is ours. We must work for the sake of the work, not for the sake of the reward, and live for others, for this life is short, and the vanities of the world are transient.

CHAPTER TWO

Jnana Yoga

Text 1: **"You have to grow from inside out. None can teach you; none can make you spiritual. There is no teacher but your own soul."**

Explanation: The quote highlights the fundamental principle of Jnana Yoga that self-realization, or the discovery of one's true nature, is a personal journey that cannot be taught or imposed from outside. Jnana Yoga is one of the paths of yoga that emphasizes the cultivation of wisdom and knowledge to attain liberation from suffering.

In Jnana Yoga, the individual is encouraged to inquire into the nature of the self and the universe to gain a deep understanding of reality. This inquiry involves introspection, reflection, and analysis of the nature of the mind, the body, and the world. The process of self-inquiry enables the individual to transcend the limitations of the ego and the intellect and merge with the infinite.

An example of Jnana Yoga from Uddhav Gita is the story of Avadhuta, a liberated soul who teaches the King Yadu about the nature of reality. Avadhuta explains that everything in the world, including the elements, the senses, and the mind, is a manifestation of the Supreme Self. He teaches that the true nature of the self is pure consciousness and that one must let go of all attachments and identities to realize it. Avadhuta exemplifies the Jnana Yogi who has attained self-realization through the path of knowledge and wisdom.

Text 2: **"You cannot believe in God until you believe in yourself."**

Explanation: This quote implies that having faith in one's own potential is a prerequisite for having faith in a higher power or God. In Jnana Yoga, this idea is related to the concept of self-knowledge or self-realization, which is considered a fundamental step in the path towards realizing the ultimate reality or Brahman.

Self-knowledge is the understanding of the true nature of the self as pure consciousness or Atman. This understanding helps an individual to transcend the limitations of the ego and the body and realize their connection with the infinite. By believing in oneself, one can cultivate the confidence and clarity needed to undertake the rigorous inquiry and introspection that is required in Jnana Yoga.

An example of this idea is the story of Swami Vivekananda, who played a key role in introducing Vedanta and Yoga to the Western world. In his early years, Swami Vivekananda struggled with self-doubt and uncertainty, which hindered his spiritual growth. However, he realized that he needed to believe in himself and his abilities to pursue the path of Jnana Yoga. With this confidence, he went on to become a renowned spiritual teacher and inspire countless people to discover their true potential. By believing in himself, Swami Vivekananda was able to realize the ultimate reality and inspire others to do the same.

Text 3: **"Man is to become divine by realizing the divine. Idols or temples, or churches or books, are only the supports, the help of his spiritual childhood."**

Explanation: In this quote, the idea is that human beings have the potential to realize their divine nature through spiritual practice and realization. The various religious practices and institutions, such as temples, churches, books, and other forms of guidance, serve as supports or aids in the process of spiritual growth and evolution.

Swami Sarvapriyananda, a contemporary spiritual teacher, explains this quote in a simple way. He suggests that the divine nature is already present within each individual, and the journey of spiritual growth is about realizing this truth. The various religious practices and institutions serve as helpful tools or supports in this process, like a ladder that helps a person climb up to reach their goal.

Swami Sarvapriyananda also emphasizes that these supports can be essential for individuals in their early stages of spiritual development. Just as children need support and guidance to learn and grow, spiritual seekers can benefit from the structure and guidance offered by religious institutions, books, or practices. However, as one progresses in their spiritual journey, these supports become less essential as the realization of the divine becomes more direct and immediate.

Overall, the quote suggests that the ultimate goal of human life is to realize our divine nature, and the various religious practices and institutions are only aids in this process. As one progresses in their spiritual journey, these supports become less necessary as the realization of the divine becomes more immediate and direct.

Text 4: **"Was there ever a more horrible blasphemy than the statement that all the knowledge of God is confined to this or that book? How dare men call God infinite, and yet try to compress him within the covers of a little book!"**

Explanation: This quote suggests that limiting one's understanding of God to a specific book or set of beliefs is a form of blasphemy, as it goes against the idea of an infinite and boundless divine reality. It is an attempt to confine the limitless nature of God within the boundaries of a limited human creation.

An example of this idea can be found in the teachings of Lord Krishna in the Bhagavad Gita. Krishna teaches that God is infinite and beyond human comprehension, and that the ultimate goal of spiritual practice is to realize the divine within oneself. He emphasizes that the divine cannot be fully understood or contained within any particular text or tradition, and that one must seek to realize the divine in one's own experience.

Krishna also teaches that the true nature of the divine is beyond human language and concepts. He uses metaphorical language and stories to convey spiritual truths, but cautions that these are only approximations of the ultimate reality. He states, "That which is the supreme Brahman, the highest abode, the imperishable, which all the Vedas declare, and which all the great sages attain, that I shall declare to you in brief: It is the unchanging, eternal, all-pervading, and supreme" (Bhagavad Gita 8.3-4).

In this way, Krishna emphasizes that the ultimate reality of God is beyond human comprehension and cannot be limited to any particular text or tradition. The true nature of the divine must be realized through direct experience, rather than through intellectual understanding or the study of texts.

Text 5: **"Each soul is potentially divine. The goal is to manifest this divinity by controlling nature, external and internal. Do this either by work, or worship, or psychic control, or philosophy – by one or more, or all of these – and be free."**

Explanation: This quote suggests that every individual has the potential to realize their innate divine nature, and that the path towards this realization involves controlling both external and internal aspects of one's being. This control can be achieved through various means, such as work, worship, psychic control, or philosophy, or through a combination of these methods.

In the Bhagavad Gita, Lord Krishna teaches the same idea, stating that every individual has a divine spark within them that can be realized through various means of spiritual practice. He teaches that by working without attachment to the fruits of one's actions, one can purify their mind and ultimately realize their divine nature. In Chapter 3, Verse 19, he states, "Therefore, without being attached to the fruits of activities, one should act as a matter of duty, for by working without attachment one attains the Supreme."

Krishna also emphasizes the importance of controlling one's mind through various forms of spiritual practice. In Chapter 6, Verse 33, he states, "For one who has conquered the mind, the mind is the best of friends; but for one who has failed to do so, his mind will remain the greatest enemy." This control can be achieved through various means, such as yoga, meditation, and other forms of spiritual discipline.

Krishna further teaches that the ultimate goal of spiritual practice is to realize one's divine nature and become free from the cycle of birth and death. In Chapter 2, Verse 45, he states, "The Vedas deal with the subject of the three modes of material nature. O Arjuna, become transcendental to these three modes. Be free from all dualities and from all anxieties for gain and safety, and be established in the self."

Overall, the quote and the teachings of the Bhagavad Gita emphasize the potential for every individual to realize their divine nature, and the importance of controlling one's external and internal nature through various means of spiritual practice in order to achieve this goal and become free.

Text 6: "**The Vedanta recognizes no sin it only recognizes error.**"

Explanation: The quote suggests that the Vedanta, a school of Hindu philosophy that emphasizes the oneness of all existence, does not view actions as inherently sinful, but rather sees them as the result of ignorance or error. This perspective recognizes that the true nature of the individual is divine and that actions are merely an expression of this divinity. Thus, the path to spiritual realization involves removing ignorance and recognizing one's true nature.

One of the most well-known teachers of the Vedanta in recent history is Sri Ramakrishna Paramhansa. He taught that the divine exists in all beings and that the ultimate goal of spiritual practice is to realize this divine nature. He also emphasized the importance of faith and devotion in the path to spiritual realization.

Ramakrishna believed that all religions lead to the same ultimate reality and that the different paths to God are simply different expressions of the same truth. He famously declared, "As many faiths, so many paths." He taught that the ultimate goal of spiritual practice is to realize the oneness of all existence and to see the divine in all beings.

Ramakrishna also emphasized the importance of love and compassion in spiritual practice. He taught that serving others and seeing the divine in all beings is an important aspect of spiritual practice. He once said, "The feeling of the Vedantist is, 'I am He.' The feeling of the bhakta is, 'He is mine.' But the ocean of Satchidananda (Existence-Knowledge-Bliss Absolute) is the same, whether you call it a tank, a pond, or a lake."

Overall, Ramakrishna's teachings emphasize the importance of recognizing the divinity within oneself and all beings, and the importance of love, compassion, and devotion in the path to spiritual realization. His teachings are in line with the Vedanta's view that actions are not inherently sinful, but rather the result of ignorance or error, and that the path to spiritual realization involves removing this ignorance and recognizing one's true nature.

Text 7: **"All knowledge that the world has ever received comes from the mind; the infinite library of the universe is in our own mind."**

Explanation: The quote suggests that all knowledge in the world originates from the human mind and that the vast library of the universe exists within our own minds. This means that our minds have the capacity to contain infinite knowledge and that we have the ability to access this knowledge through our own thinking and contemplation.

One famous quotation that supports this idea is from the ancient Indian text, the Upanishads, which states, "You are what your deep, driving desire is. As your desire is, so is your will. As your will is, so is your deed. As your deed is, so is your destiny." This quotation highlights the idea that our thoughts, desires, and actions shape our destiny, and that everything that we experience in life originates from our own minds.

In modern times, the idea that the mind is the source of all knowledge has been supported by scientific research on the brain. Studies have shown that the brain has a remarkable capacity for learning, memory, and creativity, and that these abilities stem from the vast network of neurons and connections within the brain.

Overall, the quote suggests that our minds are incredibly powerful tools for learning and knowledge, and that the key to unlocking this knowledge is through our own thinking and contemplation. By expanding our understanding of the world and ourselves, we can tap into the infinite library of the universe that exists within our own minds.

Text 8: **"All truth is eternal. Truth is nobody's property; no race, no individual can lay any exclusive claim to it. Truth is the nature of all souls."**

Explanation: The quote suggests that truth is eternal and belongs to no one individual or group. Instead, truth is a fundamental aspect of the nature of all souls and is accessible to anyone who seeks it. This means that truth cannot be owned, possessed, or controlled by any particular person or group, and that it transcends any particular culture or tradition.

This perspective is in line with the teachings of the Brahma Sutra, an ancient Indian text that explores the nature of reality and the ultimate truth. The Brahma Sutra states that the ultimate reality, known as Brahman, is the source of all creation and that it is beyond any particular individual or group. It also suggests that the ultimate goal of human existence is to realize the truth of Brahman and to merge with it.

One example from the Brahma Sutra that supports this perspective is the concept of "Neti Neti," which means "not this, not that." This concept suggests that the ultimate reality of Brahman cannot be described in words or concepts, but can only be approached through a process of negation. By recognizing what Brahman is not, we can gradually approach an understanding of what it truly is.

This approach emphasizes the importance of humility and openness in seeking the truth, and acknowledges that our own limited perspectives and experiences may not fully capture the nature of reality. By recognizing that truth is accessible to all and belongs to no one individual or group, we can remain open to new ideas and perspectives, and continue to seek the ultimate truth that transcends any particular culture or tradition.

Text 9: **"Books are infinite in number and time is short. The secret of knowledge is to take what is essential. Take that and try to live up to it."**

Explanation: The quote suggests that the amount of knowledge available in the world is vast and overwhelming, and that time is a limited resource. To gain knowledge, it is important to focus on the essential aspects of what we read, rather than trying to absorb everything. By taking what is most important, we can focus on incorporating it into our lives and putting it into practice.

One example of this principle can be found in the ancient Indian text, the Bhagavad Gita. The Gita is a vast and complex work, covering a wide range of topics related to spirituality and human existence. However, one of its most famous teachings is the concept of karma yoga, which emphasizes the importance of performing actions without attachment to the results.

While the Gita contains many other important teachings, the concept of karma yoga is seen as essential and fundamental to the overall message of the text. By focusing on this one teaching, readers can gain a deep understanding of the importance of action and detachment, and can apply this knowledge to their own lives.

In this way, the principle of taking what is essential can help readers to navigate the vast array of knowledge available in the world. By focusing on what is most important, readers can gain a deeper and more meaningful understanding of the knowledge they encounter, and can apply this knowledge to their own lives. This can help to create a more focused and purposeful approach to learning, and can help individuals to make the most of the time they have available.

Text 10: **"Desire, ignorance and inequality – this is the trinity of bondage."**

Explanation: The quote suggests that there are three key factors that keep us in a state of bondage or suffering: desire, ignorance, and inequality.

Desire refers to our attachment to material possessions and our cravings for things that we believe will bring us happiness. While there is nothing inherently wrong with having desires, our attachment to them can keep us trapped in a cycle of never-ending wants and needs, which can lead to suffering and dissatisfaction.

Ignorance refers to our lack of understanding of the true nature of reality. This can include ignorance of our own nature as spiritual beings, as well as ignorance of the interconnectedness of all things. When we are ignorant of these fundamental truths, we are more likely to be swayed by the temporary pleasures of materialistic life, and less likely to see the bigger picture of what truly matters in life.

Inequality refers to the fact that many people in the world do not have access to the basic necessities of life, such as food, shelter, and healthcare. This inequality can lead to suffering and hardship for those who are less fortunate, and can contribute to a cycle of poverty and despair.

In a materialistic life, these three factors can be particularly pronounced. The focus on acquiring material possessions can keep us trapped in a cycle of desire, while our lack of understanding of the true nature of reality can keep us in a state of ignorance. Additionally, the inequalities of the world can be magnified in a materialistic society, where those with the most resources are often able to accumulate even more at the expense of others.

To break free from this cycle of bondage, we must cultivate a deeper understanding of ourselves and the world around us. We must recognize the temporary nature of material possessions and focus on cultivating qualities such as compassion, generosity, and kindness. By doing so, we can move away from a materialistic life and towards a more fulfilling and meaningful existence that is grounded in the truth of our own divine nature.

Text 11: **"Have faith in man, whether he appears to you to be a very learned one or a most ignorant one."**

Explanation: The quote suggests that we should have faith in our fellow human beings, regardless of their apparent level of knowledge or ignorance. This is a central teaching of the Bhagavad

Gita, which emphasizes the importance of treating all beings with respect and compassion.

In Chapter 5, Verse 18, Lord Krishna says, "The humble sages, by virtue of true knowledge, see with equal vision a learned and gentle brahmana, a cow, an elephant, a dog and a dog-eater." This verse highlights the importance of seeing all beings as equal, regardless of their social status or level of education.

Similarly, in Chapter 9, Verse 29, Lord Krishna says, "I am the same to all beings; to Me there is none hateful or dear. But those who worship Me with devotion are in Me and I am also in them." This verse emphasizes the importance of recognizing the divine nature in all beings, and treating them with respect and compassion.

The Bhagavad Gita teaches that all beings are manifestations of the divine, and that we should treat them with love and kindness, regardless of their apparent level of knowledge or ignorance. By having faith in our fellow human beings, we can create a more harmonious and compassionate world, and work towards the ultimate goal of spiritual liberation.

Text 11: **"Shri Ramakrishna used to say, "As long as I live, so long do I learn." That man or that society which has nothing to learn is already in the jaws of death."**

Explanation: The quote suggests that the process of learning and growth is essential for both individuals and societies. It implies that a person or society that refuses to learn or grow is stagnating, and is at risk of decline and eventual demise.

One historical example of a society that perished due to a lack of willingness to learn is the ancient Roman Empire. The Romans were incredibly successful in the areas of law, engineering, and military conquest, and their innovations and institutions continue to influence Western society to this day.

However, despite their many achievements, the Romans were ultimately unable to adapt to changing circumstances and new challenges. They clung to traditional ways of thinking and doing things, even as their empire began to crumble around them. This rigidity and unwillingness to learn and grow contributed to their downfall.

In contrast, societies that have been willing to learn and grow, and to adapt to changing circumstances, have been more likely to thrive and succeed. For example, the United States has been successful in large part due to its ability to innovate and adapt to new challenges, including technological change, demographic shifts, and social and political upheaval.

The lesson here is that learning and growth are essential for both individuals and societies, and that a willingness to embrace new ideas and adapt to changing circumstances is key to long-term success and prosperity.

Text 12: **"The heart and core of everything here is good, that whatever may be the surface waves, deep down and underlying everything, there is an infinite basis of Goodness and Love."**

Explanation: The quote suggests that there is an underlying goodness and love in everything, despite the surface appearances. This idea is consistent with the Advaita Vedanta philosophy, which asserts that the ultimate reality, Brahman, is pure consciousness and bliss.

According to Advaita Vedanta, the universe is not fundamentally real, but rather an illusion or maya. The true nature of reality is beyond all distinctions, including good and evil. However, this does not mean that the world is devoid of goodness and love. Rather, these qualities are seen as reflections of the ultimate reality, which is pure consciousness and bliss.

In Advaita Vedanta, the path to realizing this ultimate reality involves realizing the true nature of the self, or Atman, which is identical to Brahman. This realization involves transcending the illusions of the world and recognizing the underlying unity of all things.

From this perspective, the quote suggests that even though the world may appear to be full of turmoil and negativity on the surface, the underlying reality is one of goodness and love. This goodness and love is a reflection of the ultimate reality, which is the source of all things.

Overall, the quote can be seen as an expression of the Advaita Vedanta idea that the true nature of reality is beyond all distinctions, but that this ultimate reality is reflected in the world through qualities such as goodness and love.

Text 13: **"Truth can be stated in a thousand different ways, yet each one can be true."**

Explanation: The quote suggests that truth can be expressed in many different ways, and that each expression can be valid. This idea is consistent with the Hindu philosophical tradition, which recognizes multiple paths to truth and acknowledges the validity of diverse perspectives.

Adi Shankaracharya, Shri Ramanujacharya, and Shri Madhavacharya were all important figures in the development of Hindu philosophy, and they each had their own unique perspectives on the nature of truth.

Adi Shankaracharya was a proponent of Advaita Vedanta, which asserts that the ultimate reality is Brahman, a non-dual, all-pervading consciousness. According to Shankaracharya, the world of appearances is illusory, and the true nature of reality can only be realized through the direct experience of Brahman. For Shankaracharya, truth is the realization of the non-dual nature of reality.

Shri Ramanujacharya, on the other hand, was a proponent of Vishishtadvaita Vedanta, which asserts that the ultimate reality is Brahman, but that Brahman has attributes and qualities. According to Ramanujacharya, the world of appearances is real, and the true nature of reality is the loving relationship between the individual soul and Brahman. For Ramanujacharya, truth is the experience of a personal relationship with the divine.

Shri Madhavacharya was a proponent of Dvaita Vedanta, which asserts that the ultimate reality is Brahman, but that Brahman is distinct from the individual souls and the world. According to Madhavacharya, the world of appearances is real, but it is distinct from Brahman. For Madhavacharya, truth is the experience of a loving relationship with the divine, but this relationship is one of devotion and service rather than merger or union.

Despite their different perspectives on the nature of truth, each of these philosophers recognized the validity of the others' views, and they each made important contributions to the development of Hindu philosophy. In this way, they exemplify the idea that truth can be expressed in many different ways, and that each expression can be valid.

Text 14: **"We must be bright and cheerful, long faces do not make religion."**

Explanation: This statement highlights the importance of a positive and joyful attitude in religious and spiritual pursuits. It suggests that being happy and optimistic is an essential part of being spiritual and connected to God.

For example, Hare Krishna devotees are often known for their joyful and enthusiastic chanting and dancing, which are integral parts of their spiritual practices. They believe that by expressing their love and devotion to God in this way, they can experience spiritual joy and upliftment.

In the Hare Krishna movement, the practice of sankirtan, or congregational chanting of the holy names of God, is considered the most effective method of self-realization in this age. The devotees engage in ecstatic chanting and dancing as a way to purify their hearts and minds and connect with the divine. Their bright and cheerful demeanour is a reflection of their deep faith and devotion, and is seen as an essential part of their spiritual practice.

Text 15: **"The whole universe is only the self with variations."**

Explanation: This statement is based on the Advaita Vedanta philosophy, which emphasizes the idea that the entire universe is a manifestation of the self, or Brahman. According to this philosophy, the ultimate reality is an undifferentiated oneness that is present in everything and everyone, and the apparent diversity in the world is only an illusion.

The Bhagavad Gita and Uddhav Gita are two important texts in Advaita Vedanta that discuss the concept of the self and the nature of the universe. In the Bhagavad Gita, Lord Krishna teaches that the ultimate reality is the unchanging and eternal self, which is present in all beings. He explains that the self is the source of all existence and the underlying essence of the universe.

Similarly, in the Uddhav Gita, Lord Krishna describes the self as the unchanging and eternal witness of all that exists, and explains that the universe is only a manifestation of the self. He says that the self is the only reality, and that all other things are mere illusions.

In the Vivekachudamani of Shankaracharya, the idea of the universe being a manifestation of the self is explored in depth. Shankaracharya argues that the universe is not separate from the self, but rather is an expression of its infinite nature. He emphasizes that the true self is beyond all dualities, and that the apparent diversity in the world is only a result of ignorance and illusion.

The concept of the whole universe being the self with variations is a central tenet of Advaita Vedanta, which is the school of Hindu philosophy that emphasizes the non-dual nature of reality. According to this philosophy, the ultimate reality is Brahman, an infinite, eternal, and indescribable entity that is the ground of all being. This Brahman is identical with the Atman, which is the true nature of every individual self.

Bhagavad Gita, a sacred Hindu text, highlights this concept in verse 6.29, where Lord Krishna says, "The yogi sees the Self in all beings and all beings in the Self; he sees the same everywhere." This means that for a person who has attained a state of enlightenment, the distinction between the self and the world disappears, and they see everything as an expression of the same underlying reality.

Similarly, in Uddhav Gita, Lord Krishna tells Uddhav that everything in the universe is a manifestation of the divine, and that there is no essential difference between the self and the universe. This is reflected in verses such as 11.31, where Lord Krishna says, "All this world is verily the Supreme Self, one without a second, which is of the nature of pure consciousness."

Another key text that emphasizes the non-dual nature of reality is Vivekachudamani, a philosophical treatise written by the great

Advaita philosopher Shankaracharya. In this text, Shankaracharya asserts that the self is identical with Brahman, and that the apparent diversity of the world is only an illusion. He writes, "Just as the various parts of a chariot are united in a single whole, so too is the entire universe united in the Self."

Overall, the concept that the whole universe is only the self with variations is a profound and deeply mystical idea that lies at the heart of Advaita Vedanta. It highlights the unity of all things and suggests that the true nature of reality is infinite, eternal, and ultimately indescribable.

Krishna teaches Arjuna that the self is never born and never dies, but only changes bodies, much like a person changes clothes. He explains that just as a person discards old clothes and puts on new ones, the self-discards old bodies and takes on new ones in the cycle of birth and death.

Krishna also emphasizes the importance of realizing the true nature of the self and transcending the limitations of the physical body and mind. He teaches that through yoga and self-discipline, one can attain a state of pure consciousness, or samadhi, in which the self is realized as one with the ultimate reality or Brahman.

In conclusion, the teachings of Jnana Yoga as expounded by Swami Vivekananda serve as a guiding light for seekers on the path of knowledge. Through the cultivation of discrimination, detachment and a single-pointed focus on the Self, one can attain the ultimate goal of Self-realization. Vivekananda reminds us that the true nature of the Self is infinite, eternal and beyond all dualities. By recognizing the divinity within ourselves and all beings, we can break free from the bonds of ignorance and achieve lasting peace and happiness. May these quotes inspire us to pursue the path of Jnana Yoga with unwavering dedication and steadfast devotion.

Conclusion

Swami Vivekananda's teachings on Karma Yoga and Jnana Yoga are valuable and can provide readers with a deeper understanding of life and self-realization.

In today's fast-paced world, it is easy to get caught up in the never-ending cycle of work, social obligations, and material pursuits. Swami Vivekananda's teachings on Karma Yoga and Jnana Yoga provide a powerful antidote to this way of life. By emphasizing selfless service and the pursuit of knowledge, these paths can help us attain a deeper understanding of ourselves and the universe.

Karma Yoga, also known as the path of action, teaches us the importance of performing our duties without attachment to the results. This means that we should focus on doing our best and serving others without seeking any personal gain. By doing so, we can purify our minds and achieve a state of detachment that is necessary for spiritual growth.

Jnana Yoga, on the other hand, is the path of knowledge. It emphasizes the importance of reflection, inquiry, and contemplation. By constantly reflecting on the nature of the self and the universe, we can gain a deeper understanding of the ultimate reality. This knowledge can then help us transcend the limitations of our individual ego and attain a state of oneness with the universe.

While Karma Yoga and Jnana Yoga may seem like two different paths, they are ultimately complementary. By combining selfless action with the pursuit of knowledge, we can achieve a harmonious balance between the inner and outer aspects of our lives. This balance is essential for attaining true peace and liberation.

In conclusion, I encourage readers to take the teachings of Swami Vivekananda to heart and apply them in their daily lives. By doing so, you can embark on a journey of self-discovery and spiritual growth. Whether you choose the path of Karma Yoga, Jnana Yoga, or a combination of both, may you find the inner peace and fulfilment that you seek.

ॐ सह नाववतु। सह नौ भुनक्तु। सह वीर्यं करवावहै। तेजस्वि नावधीतमस्तु। मा विद्विषावहै। ॐ शान्तिः शान्तिः शान्तिः॥

Translation: "May we be protected together, may we be nourished together, may we work together with great vigour, may our study be enlightening, and may we not hate each other. Om peace, peace, peace."

CPSIA information can be obtained
at www.ICGtesting.com
Printed in the USA
LVHW030249100623
749126LV00001B/334